Silent Messages

Dean Peiffer

BALBOA
PRESS

Copyright © 2010 Dean Peiffer

All rights reserved. No part of this book may be used or reproduced by any means, graphic, electronic, or mechanical, including photocopying, recording, taping or by any information storage retrieval system without the written permission of the publisher except in the case of brief quotations embodied in critical articles and reviews.

Balboa Press books may be ordered through booksellers or by contacting:

Balboa Press
A Division of Hay House
1663 Liberty Drive
Bloomington, IN 47403
www.balboapress.com
1-(877) 407-4847

Because of the dynamic nature of the Internet, any Web addresses or links contained in this book may have changed since publication and may no longer be valid. The views expressed in this work are solely those of the author and do not necessarily reflect the views of the publisher, and the publisher hereby disclaims any responsibility for them.

The author of this book does not dispense medical advice or prescribe the use of any technique as a form of treatment for physical, emotional, or medical problems without the advice of a physician, either directly or indirectly. The intent of the author is only to offer information of a general nature to help you in your quest for emotional and spiritual well-being. In the event you use any of the information in this book for yourself, which is your constitutional right, the author and the publisher assume no responsibility for your actions.

ISBN: 978-1-4525-0024-9 (sc)
ISBN: 978-1-4525-0025-6 (dj)
ISBN: 978-1-4525-0047-8 (e)

Library of Congress Control Number: 2010914046

Printed in the United States of America

Balboa Press rev. date:10/6/2010

to ...

Leanne

Shayna

Brianna

dreams …

visions …

Intuition …

coincidences …

omens …

These are all silent messages.

What we do with them …
Whether we listen to them,
or simply dismiss them,
Can change the course
of our lives.

When I first set out to write this, my intention was to simply share some of my own personal silent messages. A few thoughts I had received in my dreams and visions through sleeping and meditating.

It would turn out not to be that simple. I felt guided to speak a little more at length than I had originally intended. I did my best not to get too carried away with it.

My words are a reflection of my own experiences and understanding.

I've chosen to share those thoughts and feelings which resonate within myself.

It is my hope that there may be something of value here to stir your feelings within yourself.

Take then what feels right to you,
and leave the rest.

enjoy the journey ...

Namaste

Introduction

I have not always paid attention to the silent messages
in my life. I would even go so far as to say that most
often, there seemed to be none.

Of course I would be wrong.
They have always been there.

You can believe you are being guided, or not.

You can be receptive to your guidance, or not.

As I have removed a lot of the "noise" from my life,
I have become more aware and more receptive to the
silent messages
that are there for me.

This has led me to the understanding that we all are
constantly being guided by those silent messages that
surround us.

It is clear to me that the more receptive we are to our guidance, the more smoothly our lives will seem to flow.

However ... choosing to allow our silent messages to guide us will take courage. You will likely find that it's often not easy.
Therefore, it is a road less traveled. There will still be challenges to face.

You will still need to find within yourself the required strength, trust, faith, patience, and the understanding to work your way through these challenges.

There will continue to be lessons to learn. When you choose to use your courage and patience, and as you exercise more faith and trust ... these qualities will begin to grow. As you dig a little deeper ... you will find a little more.

This has been my experience in recent years.

Paying attention to the silent messages in my life has made a tremendous, positive difference.
It has helped me to be more loving with my thoughts, my words, and my actions.
I go with the natural flow of life more often.

I have more faith and trust ...
aware that I am, and will continue to be guided.

I have more patience with myself and others.

There are times of "knowing".
It's not rational thinking.
It cannot be explained.

You just know ...
And no one can tell you otherwise.

This is what I want for you.

Being receptive

It would likely seem obvious that the degree to which we are receptive to the silent messages in our lives would dictate the role they would play.
(whether major or minor)

I would suggest that our first course of action would be to remove a lot of the "noise" in our lives.

(you can read more about my thoughts on this in "moments of silence" section)

As you lessen the noise in your life, your awareness will naturally increase as you seem to receive more silent messages.

We should strive to be open-minded towards all silent messages.

Sometimes, we see only what we want to see.
This can restrict our sight and keep us from seeing what is "real".

As you work on being receptive,
try to be open to all possibilities.
Don't restrict yourself to only what you think they
should be.

Example:
If a truck cuts in front of you while you're driving, and
you respond by getting angry and beeping the horn --
while your focus is on the truck, in your frustration,
you may be missing the message on the bumper sticker
that just got put in front of your face.

Of course, one could become a bit obsessive and get
so caught up in this type of thinking ... and seemingly
find a "message" in everything.

Just relax ... be patient. They will come.

Your silent messages will be there.

As we become more aware and "receive" our messages, we will need to decide what to do with those messages …how we will react.

Maybe we won't like the messages. As always … there are choices.

We can choose to ignore them, and simply pretend they didn't happen … that they don't mean anything.

Or, we can accept them and act on them. Learning from them, allowing our silent messages to guide us in our lives and with our personal growth.

This will often take great courage … discipline … consistent efforts … trust … patience … and a "leap of faith".

Example:

I have watched a baby bird
stand on the edge of his nest,
watching the other birds flying around.

He didn't seem to know if he could fly or not.

He would continue not to know until he decided to
take that leap of faith …
to open his wings and jump.

Of course, it is his nature to fly. I knew he could do it
… that he would be fine.
But, he still had to find the courage to do it …

to take that "leap of faith".

Moments of Silence

We can all benefit tremendously by regularly choosing moments of silence in our lives.

Our lives can become very busy with seemingly no time for ourselves.

Developing the daily habit of consciously creating some quiet time for ourselves can truly be life changing.

It will help you to connect more deeply with your heart - your intuition.

This will be of great value to you. Your direction will feel more clear.

Minimizing the "noise" in your life and increasing the silence will help you to become more aware of the silent messages that surround you.

Minimizing the noise ...

Let's take a closer look at some of the "noise" that may be in our lives.

Being more aware of our habits will be the first step towards consciously creating more quiet time for ourselves.

Consider some daily choices of ours that we may not give much thought to. Choices that may be simply "out of habit".

We'll start with reflecting on the amount of time we choose to spend with our electronics. Of course this will vary from day to day.
So let's focus our attention on
what we do in general.

By electronics I'm referring to …

> television
> video games
> cell phones
> computers (internet)
> cd players
> radios
> ipods

All great tools for communicating, learning and entertainment.

All fine in moderation.

We just need to be more conscious of the amount of time we are choosing to spend here.

Let's ask ourselves a few questions …

Is it positive quality time well spent?

Is it sometimes just out of habit?

Does it have a negative impact on some of our relationships with others?

Does it feel as if our "energy" is being drained?

Is it keeping us from healthy interactions with others?

Allow me to share what I feel are some examples of unnecessary "noise" in our lives.

Surfing on the television or the internet in an attempt to find "something" to occupy our time. (maybe even while talking on the phone)

Getting involved with a long, drawn out, meaningless conversation of
blah … blah … blah …

Spending hours upon hours playing video games or sitting on the computer.

Flipping from one radio station to another or listening to the meaningless commercials.

I've seen people driving, listening to music AND talking on the phone…
all at the same time!

Too much noise!!

Again, there's nothing wrong with utilizing the tools of modern technology.
What I'm talking about is taking a closer look at the "noisy" choices that sometimes develop out of habit.

There's nothing wrong with a lengthy telephone conversation with someone you haven't spoken with in a long time or who you really enjoy exchanging "good" energy with.

But, it can be the gossip and the negative energy that can wear on you.

It's not what you do some of the time, but what you choose to do most of the time that counts.

A few things to consider …

It's ok to drive in silence

just because you own a cell phone, it doesn't need to
be "on" all the time.
(you're not "on call" unless you choose to be)

you don't need to turn on the television as soon as
you wake up, or right when you
walk in the door.

and … you definitely don't need it entertaining you as
you're lying in bed,
right before you go to sleep.

please …

please …
minimize the noise.

Just try it ...

You'll be glad you did,
as you begin to enjoy
more of the silent messages
around you.

Let's talk about creating or simply allowing moments of silence into our lives.

Nature...

Spending time in nature is a great, very natural way to enjoy moments of silence.

This could be as simple as spending time
in your own backyard
(depending how quiet it is)
or
at a park going for a walk in the woods, camping, hiking.
More choices include spending time at the beach, by a river, pond, or stream.

There's just something about spending some quiet time in nature that seems to connect us to the "bigger picture"… the universe.

If you feel the need to take your phone with you, try to leave it turned off. Otherwise, leave it at home. It's ok - they'll leave a message.

You may notice that after you've spent some time relaxing quietly in nature, that you will feel more of a sense of calm.

Sometimes, you may suddenly have a revelation as to how to handle a situation that you've been trying to work through.

You may also have some creative ideas that seem to just come to you.

Maybe how you feel about things that might have been on your mind will become more clear.

… these are silent messages.

Sleep ...

Sleep … what better way to take some quiet time …
some would say "there's not"!

Good quality sleep is an extremely important part of
our daily lives …

regular, sufficient sleep…
(waking up naturally without the alarm clock)
will lend itself towards feeling well-rested.

add in a little nutrition
and you are able to enjoy
a good quality of life
with plenty of energy,

and …

... if you are so inclined,
feel free to treat yourself to a nap.

I've heard one satisfied customer once refer to naps as
being "fun".

Even the shortest ones may help to rejuvenate you so
you can remain fully alert
during your waking hours.

Sleep ... at all stages,
will naturally lend itself to
dreams and visions,
and the possibility of
waking with an idea,
a thought, or a "knowing".

... all silent messages.

Meditation ...

"Most importantly
before anything else …
meditate."

(words I actually received during meditation)

If you're not already doing it, I would like to strongly encourage you to develop a consistent daily practice of meditation.
Simply sit in silence.

It will help you to be more aware of and more receptive to your silent messages.

(The following words came to me in a dream…)

"The meditation session needs to be honored and respected.
People should feel that they want to be part of it …
that it's their choice."

Of course, there are many ways to meditate …

laying, sitting, walking, various forms of chanting and guided visualizations, etc.

I would suggest that you experiment with the various forms, and go with the one
that works for you.

… choose whatever best helps you to focus and calm your "mind chatter".

Whatever you choose, finding the time for meditation may be the single, most valuable habit you can develop for yourself,
as you move towards being more connected with your own silent messages.

The following words were an intuitive response from me to another seeking some guidance …

"taking some quiet time for yourself will lead you to the understanding that the answers to all of your questions lie within yourself."

Sit in silence
sounds simple … and it is.
but, it's going to take some effort.

You will need to be …

Consistent - daily practice should be the goal.

Patient - it will seem easier some days than others.

Persevere - hang in there you can do it!

Please ...
be patient with yourself and the process.

Do your best to dismiss any frustrations or
intimidations that may arise.

Remember your goal ...
the quiet connection with

Your inner self
Your higher self
The universe
Your soul
God
collective consciousness

(whatever you comfortably relate to)
(whatever feels "right" to you)

As you develop the daily habit of taking some quiet time for yourself, it will be best to be consistent with your practice.

Begin with something that's doable ...
as little as a few minutes if you need to.

Initially, your focus is on creating the habit. At the start of your day would be best.
However, it would be most important to choose a time of day that you are willing to be consistent with.
(you may find better results with this approach rather than just trying to fit it in whenever.)

There will always be benefit to any efforts you make towards connecting with your inner self ... and your silent messages.

Some people have a concern about falling asleep while sitting in silence.

There would seem to be an advantage here in the seated position. Laying down to meditate may lend itself towards the more likely possibility of falling asleep.

I personally have fallen asleep
in the seated position.
But, the way I see it,
even if you do fall asleep
it was not a waste of your time.
You were successfully able to quiet your mind.

again … the goal is silence.

At times, while meditating, you may feel as if you did not fall asleep, but you really were not "awake" either. You found yourself somewhere "in-between."

... Just allow what "is" to "be".

(The following is from "A Course in Miracles")

"Sit quietly and close your eyes.
The light within you is sufficient.
It alone has power to give
the gift of sight to you.
Exclude the outer world, and
let your thoughts fly to the peace within.
They know the way"

Relax … and close your eyes.

As you sit in silence, there will be times that your mind will attempt to "entertain" you with a variety of thoughts.

This may be a list of things you recently accomplished. Possibly, a list of things to do. Maybe any issues you may currently be dealing with.
It may even try to predict the future.

Simply smile and tell it "no thank you."
It can be a challenge. It likely won't be easy.
It will seem easier some days than others.
That's ok … It's still worthwhile.
Try not to get frustrated.

Be patient with yourself.
It will take practice.
Be consistent with your efforts.

I have found it to be quite helpful
to focus on my breath in an effort to
quiet the "mind chatter."
A slow, deliberate inhale ... then exhale.
You may try this with little or no success.
Your mind is very clever.

It is worth mentioning again to be patient with
yourself and consistent with your efforts.
In time, with practice,
it will become more doable.
There will be days that sitting for five minutes will feel
like an hour. And other days, that hour will seem like
five minutes.
Allow it to be as it is.
Do your best and be content with that.
Then ... move about your day.

I have been sitting in silence for many years. It took me a long time, and a lot of patience and effort before I "got something".

I was once advised to allow "it" to come to me … and not to "go after it".
This has proven to be good advice.
Try not to have any expectations.

You may ask yourself …
how do you know the difference
between a "message" and wishful thinking?
In other words … how do you know that you did not create the whole thing in your mind?

All I can simply say here is …
You will have a "knowing."
You will just know.

It is my opinion that disappointment, frustration, and anger will hinder your receptiveness to your silent messages.

It will be very exciting to see "lights" and "visions". Similar to dreams, they may be moving, like a movie. Or, they may be still like a photograph. Occasionally, you may hear a voice or get goose bumps. You may smell something familiar. Try not to get too excited. Stay relaxed, receptive, and observe. You may actually find this easy to do, as you will likely be in a "zone". Being in a zone will automatically lend itself towards more focus. Once you "get something" and then as you continue your daily practice you find that you "get nothing." <u>Do not be discouraged!</u> Be patient. Again ... this is not entertainment. Keep your ego out of it.
These silent messages are from your guidance. Give it the respect it deserves.

Apply those messages that you do receive
to your life.

The more you do this ...
the more you'll get.

A word on "goose bumps".

For me, when I get goose bumps,
it has been a clear indication of
the presence of Spirit.

A word on "multiple messages"…

At times, I've received multiple visions or messages
during a meditation session.
It has been my experience,
that it can be very challenging -
even impossible to try to remember
what I have "received", <u>and</u>
continue to sit in silence with a "quiet" mind.

I feel that when you do receive messages …
you should write them down.
(We should not ignore our silent messages) Then,
make the choice whether or not
to return to meditating.

Note:
I have received multiple messages,
decided to come out of sitting to write them down,
then returned to my meditative state … only to receive
more.
It doesn't always work that way …
but, it can happen.

Since you are reading this …
I know that you are looking for "guidance"… your own personal silent messages.

When they come, and I promise you they will, you must really do your best at receiving
what you are given.
You should not act as if you didn't see them,
or hear them, or feel them.
Maybe you did not get exactly what you were
"looking" for … what you had in mind …
or what you were hoping for.
But that's what I mean about
opening your heart, your ears, your mind, and being receptive to that which you do receive.

We don't know the "bigger picture".

Some of our toughest lessons are
patience and trust.
Trusting that things truly will unfold
in our best interest
(as they always are.)
… in the manner and time frame
that is most appropriate for us.

<u>Really Trust That</u> !!

Be patient. Just take it one day at a time. Maybe even
… one hour at a time.
Try not to look too far ahead.

Your mind will want to entertain you with various
possibilities and probabilities.
Again … there will be days that you may see lights and
visions - possibly hear a voice. Other days, the best
you can hope for
is to quiet your mind a bit.

I want to remind you to <u>be content with that</u> !

Any efforts you give towards sitting in silence and
quieting your mind will prepare you to being more
receptive to your silent messages … in any and all
forms that they come to you.

Once you can "check" your ego,
your quiet confidence will allow you to
sit in silence daily …
content with the silence itself …
regardless of whether or not
you "get something"

You will have a quiet understanding …
a "knowing" that you will get what you need when the
time is right.

(Actual vision received while meditating)

There was an empty water bottle standing upright in space. I had another one in my hand and flipped it (end-over-end) through the air. I watched as it landed open-end down,
and fell perfectly right into the other one.
(I felt myself physically jerk back in astonishment, with this big smile on my face, with the understanding that I had just witnessed "the impossible".)

My Interpretations….

<u>Anything</u> is possible.

You could try all day to force the one bottle into the other, and would never get anywhere.
Yet, if not forced, things magically
fall into place perfectly.

Trying to force the situation, you will not get anywhere. Simply allow things to perfectly "fall" into place naturally.

Dreams ...

Dreams ... we all have them.
Some of us are more aware of them than others.
Dreams are obviously
very valuable silent messages.

I feel it's worth taking the time and effort to write down as many of your dreams as possible ... no matter how crazy they may seem.

If you wake up and are aware that you had a dream, but don't want to be bothered with writing it down because you'll remember it later ... think again. This is rarely the case.

You should try to record them in a quick and immediate manner, as soon as possible.

Include your thoughts and feelings from the dream with as many details as possible, including colors, numbers, etc.

Sometimes, I write so fast, when I go back later, I can't read my own writing.

So ... another piece of advice.
If you're going to take the time to write it down, you might as well take the time to write it
so you'll be able to read it.
Write as fast and as legible as you can.
Again ... getting down the main ideas and important details as quickly as possible,
along with any immediate interpretations
you may have.

Note:
There have been times that I have foregone writing down the actual dream, and have simply written the interpretation.
(Sometimes it's that clear to me.)

How you choose to record your dreams
is up to you ... Whatever works for you.
If you're going to write them down, having a pen and
paper immediately available is essential, along with
minimum light ...
just enough to see ... maybe a night light
or a candle.

So ... once you realize you had the dream and you
want to write it down ...
Every minute Is Valuable !

You don't want to be turning on bright lights and
running around looking for something to write on and
something to write with.

It's interesting ... sometimes I'll wake in the morning
and look to see what I wrote with absolutely no
memory at all of the dream
I wrote about. Other times,
I smile ... as I have instant recollection.

At times you will find that, as you go back
to rewrite your dreams,
giving them additional thought,
you will have some insight
as to what the "messages" mean to you …
and how they relate to what's currently
going on in your life.

Your dreams are always about you
regardless of who is in your dream.

There may not always be a deep meaning
or an easy interpretation …
but, try asking yourself …
If you had to come up with a meaning
what would it be?

Try to give meaning to your own dreams
before looking for interpretations
through other sources. (books, internet, etc)

It may help to share your dreams with someone else.
They may have some insight that may be of some
benefit to you …
another way to interpret your message.
Maybe it was just meant to get your attention, and
remind you that you're not alone.

I've noticed that the more I write them down, the more I seem to get ...
the more understanding I seem to have regarding their meaning
and how they may apply to my life.

It is not unusual to receive
a similar message repeatedly.

I've always felt that when you seem to
hit a "dry spell"
one should continue to focus
on the last dream received ...
making a sincere attempt to apply its message into your life.

Dreams can happen at any time
during sleep state.
I've already had them within
the first hour or two.
Many seem to come in the last couple of hours, but
they've also happened
everywhere in between.

I'm sure they may even happen during a nap …
even an "unscheduled" one, when you
just happen to "doze" off.

My final thoughts are this …

I do not pretend to possess the ability to be able to interpret and understand all of my dreams. But … there are times when their meaning is quite clear.
At this point it is "message received".

If you want the messages to have more value than simply entertainment purposes,
you will need to give some efforts towards applying them to your life.

This is a path of learning … a path of growth.

It's not always easy or convenient, but it will always be worth your time and efforts.
So … be patient with yourself.
Be consistent. Persevere.

Our silent messages are our communications to help us along our path.

The following are a couple of examples
of dreams of mine.

Included are the notes
along with interpretations.

I made a large black and white sketch
of a man meditating from the waist up.
As I was looking at it, it started moving …
like it was real!
So, this guy walks over and he starts looking at it with
me. He asked "What did you make?" I said "He's
meditating".
We're looking at it as I see it moving … again! So does
the other guy! He sees it, too!
He looks at me in disbelief.
I said "It's wiggin me out" and he starts laughing at
what I said.
He's lying on the floor laughing.

My interpretation:

What I'm writing will come to life
or …
take on a life of its own.

I was in the hallway of a school.
And although I was a personal trainer,
I was not training at the time.
So I was asked by someone in charge to guide a new teacher to her mailbox.
Hers was the section on top. It was packed full. There were a lot of papers.
As I started to pull them out, I noticed a couple of books … that's where my focus went to.

My interpretation:

When I'm not working as a personal trainer
I need to recycle papers into something of value to help others.
My focus should be on a couple of books.

"Allow yourself to be guided"
I was driving along down a hill when I found myself driving through water,
(small river or large creek)
finding spots that are not too deep ... the most shallow. Not too far ahead of me was this beautiful waterfall (wide and high).
As I continued driving, getting closer to the waterfall, the water seemed to be getting deeper and moving faster. I thought about turning around, but then it was as if I could see more clearly, and more shallow areas started presenting themselves to me.
So I carefully proceeded. I felt that I would get through ok. It would not be much further.

My interpretation:

Allow myself to be guided.
Keep moving forward.
I will continue to see more clearly.

Visions ...

When I speak of a vision,
I consider it to usually be a "still" message,
received at any time, but most often while sleeping or
during meditation.

As opposed to a dream being more like watching a
movie, a vision would be more like
looking at a photograph.
(It could also be just a name, a word,
a group of words, a number, etc.)

This "still" message can be a simple,
yet very powerful silent message.
At times, I've had one … maybe two.
But, I've had as many as six at a time.

Note:
I've noticed that when I receive these messages in
groups, they seem to have a common thread that ties
them together.
They kind of tell a story … a larger message.

Actual vision received during meditation.

(it was like looking at a photograph.)

Three pink flamingos
each standing on one leg
painted on the side of a white van.

My interpretation:

As I move along my journey
currently there is good balance in my life.

Actual phrase received …
"God is on call"

My interpretation:
Literal … always available

Actual word received …
"diatribe"

My reaction:
A word I am not familiar with.
I looked it up in the dictionary.
Then spent some time trying to figure out how that
fits into what's going on in my life.

Actual thought received …
"I just need to put it out there
and not be so concerned with
how it ties in with everything else."

Intuition ...

When I speak of "following your heart",
I'm referring to listening to your inner self ... your intuition.
At times you will instinctively have ...
a feeling
an understanding
a knowing
I consider this your intuition.
It very likely cannot be rationally explained
or proven ... it just is.
you sense it
you feel it
you just know it

These silent messages may come from the Universe,
your Guidance, your Higher Self, your Soul.
I'm not really sure where they come from, and ... I'm
not really sure it matters.
But, I do know that the more you
trust your instincts, your intuition,
these silent messages,
the easier your life will seem to flow.

Coincidences ...

I consider coincidences to be events
that just seem to happen with perfect timing … often
in an unforeseeable, surprising, unexplainable manner.
We may be aware of them … we may not.
They are not "accidents".
They are silent messages.

They could be …

Money that shows up in your life
just when you need it.

A person who calls as you were
recently thinking of them.

An obvious question answered
by someone who is unaware of your pondering.

Someone suggests a way to handle a
situation you've found yourself in …
and it makes perfect sense to you.

I feel that it's so important to pay close attention to
those things that
"just seem to happen",
or those things or people who seem to
show up at just the right time.

The more open-minded and receptive you are … the
more you give it your "energy",
the more you will get.

You may sometimes notice the same thing reoccurring
… it could be …
a number
a name
a song

Maybe there is a specific silent message there
or
maybe it's just a reminder
that you are not alone.

Omens ...

I view an omen as something you may hear
or see that may have a special,
significant meaning to you.
It will likely mean nothing at all
to anyone else.

It's as if the Universe is speaking to you
and everyone else is unaware.

The author Paulo Coelho,
who wrote "The Alchemist", once described "omens"
during an interview.
It would be most appropriate for me to share
his words with you now …

"Omens are the individual language
in which God talks to you.
My omens are not your omens.
They are this strange, but
very individual language that guides you toward your
own destiny.
They are not logical.
They talk to your heart directly.
The only way that you can learn any language is by
making mistakes.
I made my mistakes, but then I started to connect with
the signs that guide me.
This silent voice of God that leads me
to the places where I should be."

Final Thoughts ...

So … being receptive to our silent messages
and allowing them to guide us,
really can help to change our lives for the better

… allowing us to be more positive
and more loving in our thinking,
our speaking, and our actions.

Helping us to find more patience
and understanding
with ourselves and others.

So … open your mind and open your heart
as you continue your journey.

With Great Love …
Namaste,
Dad

Messages received ...

The following are a collection of my thoughts and
feelings from my own dreams, meditations and
moments of insight.

They have helped to guide me
along my journey.
They may be of some value to you as well.

Some may seem redundant,
Others ... vague or unclear.

Again, I'm sharing some of the messages I received ...
that obviously have spoken to me.

However ... I have chosen to share them with you,
with the understanding that possibly there may be
something of value
in these words for you as well.

Time to awaken.
Get up.

The torch has been lit.
Another month or two.
A butterfly fluttering.

Time to mend fences …
fix what needs to be fixed.
It needs to be secure.
Do what you need to do.

Give attention to that which needs attention …
do it now.

There is help.
Working together…
The time has come.

Follow your heart.

You'll have a "knowing" …
Just follow your heart

Keep the "light" on.
Be patient.
Pace yourself.
It's an ongoing journey.

Be positive …
Be patient.
You really don't know about the "business" of the Universe (the bigger picture).
Find something to occupy your time with.

Trust, that with time
it will all be ok.

As you walk
out of the darkness
and into the light …
things will become more clear.

Surrender to the
natural flow of life.

Follow guidance.
<u>Trust guidance</u>
even if it doesn't seem right.
Don't fight it.
go with the
"natural" flow of things.

Not all of the various "circumstances" and
"delays" that you are faced with
along your journey
are about <u>you</u>.

Stay calm and in the moment.

Allowing the natural flow
of things to unfold
may not have anything to do with <u>you.</u>

"Things just have a
way of working out."

"You gotta believe."

Everything can change
in an instant.

Change can happen
<u>really quick</u>!
<u>Unbelievably quick</u>!!

" Do the right thing …
at the right time …
for the right reasons … "

Be more aware of your words …
your words leave impressions.

"At the banquet of life …
sit up and eat."

Be creative …
Have fun …
Enjoy life …

Do what you know is right …
Find a way !

You continue to know
what's right for you
by how you <u>feel</u>.

You will be taken care of.
You just need to be patient.
It's a natural process
that takes time.
It's not just about "you" …
other people have needs too.

Just like the stars …
there is perfect order
in the world.

Things will "line up" just right when they
are meant to.
Then it will all be
very clear to you.

In the game of life
you're being given
what you need.
So you can do
what you need to do.

What you want, along with what's good
(best) for you,
will be put in your hands.

Follow the guidance you get.

Keep sharing with others.

Try not to water it down ...
"give it" as you "get it".

Spirit will come to you
wherever you are.

Do everything you can
to stay connected to Spirit.

Timing is just not right.

Try not to be frustrated.

Be patient.

Don't try to force <u>your</u> way
or a situation onto others … work more
<u>with</u> them.

go with the natural flow
of things.
You'll get there either way.

It will be much easier
on everyone
if you are less controlling and just go with
the flow.

Stay the course.
Stay focused.

Help teach others.

Life is a series of
ups and downs.

" around here, all life
goes in cycles. "

When life moves …
move with it.

Even a small action
that may only take a minute, can make a
nice difference.

In the caring is the understanding.

Even with the most
challenging of situations,
you can get through it ...
but it might require a little creativity,
effort, and sacrifice.

Hang in there ...

You can run,
but you can't hide.
You are who you are.

Be honest …
just be who you are…
and live your truth …
while allowing others
to be who they are,
and live their truth.

When you face your fears
they will no longer be "fears".

They'll have no power over you … <u>none</u> !

They're not real.

They cannot survive once you face them.

You may need to
give something up
in order to achieve what you
are really looking for.

Be willing to let things go ...
then, you will have them.

Sort through things
and thoughts for that
which has value.

get rid of what is not needed.

Clean yourself up,
get rid of what is not needed.

It's a slow process ...
not easy !

but ... it's going to
make a nice difference.

well worth your
time and effort.

When blockage is removed
things can move quickly.

Be cautious to do
all that you can to prevent the "fires" in
your life …
(that which has the ability to cause
destruction and destroy)
… from returning

the way to stop the " burning "
is to go to the core.

Do not intentionally
mislead others ...
you wouldn't like it.

Be careful.
Don't take careless chances. Trust your
instincts.

When considering
instant gratification
in a moment of weakness …
dig deep to find the strength you need to
be patient.

You will be glad you held out.

When you realize that you are being
tempted or challenged …
simply remove yourself
from the situation.

Think ahead …

We create our own "problems" by our behavior and choices.

Often times, we are able to control our "circumstances"
and not put ourselves in the situation of needing to eliminate something.

Wash your hands
of the situation,
thought process, or behavior.

Continually eliminate that which is no
longer necessary …
you will know.

When it seems as if
the odds are against you,
and by all appearances there's just no way
you can win …
but you do.

despite appearances …
<u>all things truly are possible !</u>

Stay connected to your soul
to see you through.

Don't be so distracted
by appearances
that you don't
see what's "real".
(the truth)

Despite appearances …
things do <u>not</u> always go
the way that they
<u>seem</u> they will.

You are healing …
and have support
always available to you
as you follow the path
that you choose.

Allow yourself to be guided.

you will think more clearly
and
you will see more clearly.

glimpse of hope
in the distance …
(in the future)

you're not always
able to see it …
but it's there.

Nothing lasts forever …

recognize and appreciate
the efforts of others

You _know_ what to do.

" The perception will be
that there are judgments,
which may or may not be true.

you just need to be as
fair as you possibly can
and go with that …

just do your best."

About the author

Dean Peiffer has become increasingly more aware of his own silent messages through personal meditations, dreams and moments of insight. He continues to receive his silent messages while living in the Northeastern United States where he is able to personally share them with his children, grandchildren and others.

www.ingramcontent.com/pod-product-compliance
Lightning Source LLC
Chambersburg PA
CBHW020009050426
42450CB00005B/376